HOW TO
COMMUNICATE
EFFECTIVELY
and
HANDLE
DIFFICULT PEOPLE

by Preston C. Ni, M.S.B.A.

Burgess Publishing

A Division of Burgess International Group, Inc.

Also by Preston C. Ni
WITH DIGNITY AND HONOR
Understanding Racism, Unlearning Racism

Write to the author at:

pcn2231@mercury.fhda.edu

Copyright © 1999 by Preston Che Ping Ni

ISBN 0-8087-6580-9

Printed in the United States of America.
J I H G F E D C B A

Address orders to:

BURGESS INTERNATIONAL GROUP, Inc.
7110 Ohms Lane
Edina, Minnesota 55439-2143
Telephone 612-820-4561
Toll Free 1-800-356-6826
Fax 612/831-3167

Burgess Publishing
A Division of BURGESS INTERNATIONAL GROUP, Inc.

❧ DIVIDENDS FOR LIFE ❧

Our deepest fear is not that we
are inadequate.

Our deepest fear is that we are powerful
beyond measure.

It is our light, not our darkness, that most
frightens us.

We ask ourselves, who am I to be brilliant,
gorgeous, talented, and fabulous?

Actually, who are you NOT to be?

You are a child of the universe.

Your playing small doesn't serve the world.

There's nothing enlightened about shrinking
so that other people won't feel insecure
around you.

We were born to manifest the glory that is
within us.

It's not just in some of us; it's in everyone.

As we let our own light shine, we
unconsciously give other people permission
to do the same.

As we are liberated from our own fear, our
presence automatically liberates others.

—*quoted by Nelson Mandela*
1994 Inaugural Speech

How to
Communicate Effectively
and
Handle Difficult People

≋ Table of Contents ≋

INTRODUCTION BY JOSÉ MARIA J. YULO   9

FUNDAMENTAL HUMAN RIGHTS   11

EIGHT LEVELS OF ASSERTIVENESS   12

CHAPTER ONE   INEFFECTIVE COMMUNICATION   13
- **"You" Language Plus Directives**
- **Universal Statements**
- **Tough on the Person, Soft on the Issue**
- **Invalidate Feelings**

CHAPTER TWO   EFFECTIVE COMMUNICATION   19
- **"I" Language**
- **Specificity and Consequence**
  - *How to Get Evidence*
  - *How to Set Consequence*
- **Soft on the Person, Tough on the Issue**
  - *How to be Soft on the Person*
  - *How to be Tough on the Issue*
  - *Using "You" Language to be Soft on the Person*
  - *Using "You" Language in the Form of a Question*
  - *Using "You" Language to Interrupt a Show of Disregard*
- **Listen and Validate Feelings**

CHAPTER THREE   POWER ASSERTION SKILLS: THE ART OF
HANDLING DIFFICULT PEOPLE   31

- Definition and Cautions
- Pick Your Battles
- Staying Cool/The True Nature Behind Difficult and
  Aggressive Behavior
- Keeping Yourself Grounded
- Powerful Body Language, Words and Tone of Voice
- Humor and Sarcasm

  Three Ways to Use Humor and Sarcasm

  *Possible Reactions From Difficult or Aggressive People
  When You Use Humor and Sarcasm*

CHAPTER FOUR   CONFLICT RESOLUTION:
A STEP-BY-STEP GUIDE   43

- Problem Statement
- Understanding the Nature of Power

  Two Categories of Power

  Seven Specific Types of Power

- Power Dynamic Analysis
- Dealing with Predominately Emotional Situations

  If You Have More Emotional Power

  *If You Both have Significant Emotional Power
  Over Each Other*

  If the Other Person Has More Emotional Power

- Dealing with Predominately Tangible Situations

  If You Have More Tangible Power

  *If You Both Have Significant Tangible Power
  Over Each Other*

  If the Other Person Has More Tangible Power

- Brainstorm Solutions
- Identify Solution

A NOTE OF APPRECIATION   61

≋ Introduction ≋

A question that I often ask my students in communication is, "What do you think intelligence is?" Though the answers to this query mirror the variety and complexity of today's student body, there resonates, above the din, a common sentiment.

In keeping with our modern, multicultural society, students no longer insist on mere checklists of facts and figures as gauges of intelligence. Although a broad and deep understanding of ideas is integral, the ability to communicate these thoughts and feelings has gained equal importance.

It is this new idea of communicative intelligence that Mr. Preston Ni champions in his book.

Here, he advocates the challenging and fulfilling practice of assertive communication—a practice of strongly yet peaceably defending and defining one's self in the midst of human conflict. Along with this, Mr. Ni takes on the daunting task of communicating with those among us who are not predisposed to effective communication. His methods of dealing with "difficult people" are revealing and serve as good insurance for us as our world gets more and more diverse. These methods will help to quell some of the negative feelings that arise from a society's rapid change.

As the definition of intelligence evolves into more pragmatic forms, so does Mr. Ni's treatment of his topics. He covers his material both comprehensively and efficiently, giving the reader down-to-earth suggestions and solutions in dealing with even the most complicated situations and people.

The generous scope that Mr. Ni lends to the issues is a testament to his mettle as a teacher. It allows other to see his sensitivity to what students are well aware of—What it is to be intelligent.

José Maria J. Yulo
Department of
Speech Communication
Foothill College
Los Altos Hills, Callifornia

FUNDAMENTAL HUMAN RIGHTS

We have these rights as long as we do not harm others. If we harm other people, then we forfeit our right to have these rights.

1. We have the right to be treated with respect.

2. We have the right to express our feelings, opinions, and wants.

3. We have the right to be listened to and taken seriously.

4. We have the right to set our own priorities.

5. We have the right to say "no" without feeling guilty.

6. We have the right to get what we pay for.

7. We have the right to have our opinions different than others.

8. We have the right to take care of and protect ourselves from being threatened physically, mentally or emotionally.

In the United States, our Constitution, our Bill of Rights, our civil rights, our democratic process and our consumer protection laws assume these rights for all, regardless of our sex, culture, age, religion or class. Although some people in our society do not respect these rights, *in the United States we have the right to fight for these rights.*

More importantly, we have these rights because **we say so.** If we believe we are worthy and deserving of respect, then we will live our lives and conduct ourselves accordingly. If we do not believe we are worthy of these rights, then we have lost no matter what measure of protection society brings us.

This book can help you gain the necessary skills to stand up for yourself and assert your Fundamental Human Rights.

Eight Levels Of Assertiveness in the Face of Difficult or Aggressive People

Level	Characteristics	Possible States of Being
8. Victim	Do nothing. Suffer in silence.	Fear, Hurt, Powerlessness
7. Victim	Passive aggressive, indirectly express displeasure.	Fear, Anger, Resentment
6. Stand-Up	Ineffective arguing.	Anger, Blame, Judgment
5. Stand-Up	Win over others. Survival of the fittest.	Win/Lose
4. Stand-Up	Win others over. Win respect from friends as well as foes.	Win/Win
3. Prevention	Stop others' negative behavior early on.	Awareness, Power Assertion Skills
2. Prevention	Prevent negative behavior from happening at all, just by your presence.	Consciousness, Charisma
1. Transformation	Your presence automatically transforms others for the better, melts away fears and anxieties. Love and compassion as forms of strength and power.	Consciousness, True love

CHAPTER ONE

Ineffective Communication

Ineffective communication is the type of communication which is likely to cause conflict and defensiveness. This type of communication often worsens relationships.

"You" Language and Directives

Ineffective communication is often characterized by the use of certain types of "you" language, such as "you are. . .," "you should. . .," "you need to. . .," "you have to. . .," "you'd better. . .," and "you people. . . ." *Directives* are statements which order another person around. Some examples of "you" language with a directive include:

> "You need to go do this now. . ."
>
> "You people should behave. . ."
>
> "You have to understand my position. . ."
>
> "You really ought to know by now that. . ."

Most of us don't like to be told what to do, and when we use "you" language plus a directive, it's easy to arouse in other people feelings of resentment and defensiveness. This type of communication is also problematic in that they tend to invite a "no" response, often resulting in disagreements and conflicts.

There are effective ways of getting your point across clearly and successfully without using "you" language and directives. There are also other types of "you" language that are effective to use. We will examine all of these in chapter two.

Universal Statements

Universal statements are statements that generalize a person's character or behavior in a negative way. The most common types of universal statements involve the use of words such as "always," "never," "again," "so," "every time," "such a," and "everyone." Universal statements are often used in combination with "you" language. For example:

> "You *always* leave the toilet seat up."

> "You *never* put the tooth paste cap back on."

> "You're messing up *again!*"

> "You are *so* lazy!"

> "You forget to do this *every* time!"

> "You're *such a* slob!"

> "*Everyone* knows that you're bad."

Universal statements are problematic in many ways. First, the inherent message within these statements is that, in the mind of the person who speaks such generalizations, there is no possibility of the other person being anything else. Second, because universal statements tend to point out "what is wrong," instead of "how to be better," such statements discourage change. Finally, just as with examples of "you" language earlier, universal statements can easily be disputed. If I say to you, "you never wash the dishes,"all you need to do is to come up with *one* exception, "that's not true, Preston, I washed the dishes once last year," and you have successfully contradicted my statement. The general nature of universal statements makes them very vulnerable to specific counterexamples.

Universal statements are essentially over-generalized, negative judgments. It is especially important to avoid using universal statements when communicating with children, as such statements can negatively affect their self-esteem. In chapter two, we will cover many effective ways of communication with children as well as adults.

Tough on the Person,
Soft on the Issue

In every communication situation involving another person, there are two elements present: the person you are relating to, and the issue or behavior you are addressing. Effective communicators know how to separate the issue or the behavior from the person, and be soft on the person and tough on the issue. Ineffective communicators will do the opposite. They literally "get personal" by being tough on the person, while minimizing or ignoring the issue or the behavior.

For example:

Ineffective communication: "You are so stupid!"
Effective communication: "You're a smart person, and* what you did this morning was not very smart."

Ineffective communication: "You never clean up. You're a slob!"
Effective communication: "I noticed that you didn't wash the dishes this week."

Ineffective communication: "You are a poor student."
Effective communication: "You can do well in this class, and I noticed that you got a "C" on your last exam."

Being tough on the person and soft on the issue can easily arouse negative reactions from people who are likely to take what you're saying more personally, and as a result feel angry, resentful, hurt or resistant. Note that tough on the person and soft on the issue also involves the frequent use of "you" statements and universals.

*It is better to use "and" instead of "but" in certain situations. "But" is a **negator** which can discount the significance of what is said before and puts the real meaning of the sentence on what comes after. (I like you as a friend, but. . . .) "Yes, but. . ." often times means "no." So if you don't mean to negate the first part of your sentence, use "and" instead of "but." "And" is a **connector** which places equal emphasis on both what is said before and after.

Invalidate Feelings

Invalidation of feelings occurs when we recognize emotions, positive or negative, coming out of a person, and either discount, belittle, minimize, ignore or negatively judge these feelings.

For example:

> "Your concerns are meaningless to me!"

> "Your complaints are totally unfounded."

> "You're blowing things way out of proportion."

> "Your anger is a big over-reaction."

> "So what if you got a B in math? I used to get A's all the time."

> "I don't have time for a hug right now, sweetie. Now go wash up for dinner!"

When we invalidate another person's feelings, we are likely to cause *instant resentment.* The person (or group) whose feelings we just invalidated is likely to feel hurt and angry. In some cases, a person whose feelings have been invalidated might shut down from you emotionally, so that her/his feelings will not be hurt again. Invalidation of emotions is one of the most destructive things one can do in close, personal relationships. It is one of the main reasons why "fall outs" occur between friends, family and people in intimate relationships.

CHAPTER TWO

Effective Communication

In this chapter we will look at communication skills that are critical in communicating effectively with people on a daily basis. These are also the skills that can help you stand up for yourself and exercise your fundamental human rights (as listed on page 11 in this book).

Properly used, these *effective communication skills* can help you get along with people ninety to ninety-five percent of the time. The other five to ten percent are those instances when you encounter people who are very difficult to deal with. We will discuss how to deal with difficult people in chapter three.

"I" language

Examples of "I" language include:

"I think. . ."

"I believe. . ."

"I want. . ."

"I feel. . ."

"I won't. . ."

"I refuse to. . ."

"I prefer that. . ."

"It is important to me that. . ."

"I don't appreciate it when. . ."

"I would appreciate it if. . ."

"It doesn't work for me to. . ."

"It is unacceptable to me that. . ."

"It is inappropriate for me to. . ."

"I" language is often an effective method of communicating. It is more difficult to say "no" to "I" statements than "you" language. At the most, "I" language tends to invite a "why?"

response, which is less oppositional and allows you to discuss an issue further.

Evidence and Consequence

Effective communication often involves the use of evidence, backed up at times with consequence.

Evidence is comprised of the specifics of an issue. *Consequence* is what you are willing to do given the situation.

Please note the following formula:

Specific evidence + consequence = the power to back up your communication.

How to get evidence

You can get evidence by:

A. Collecting and examining all the facts related to the situation, including what, where, when, why, how and whom.

B. Collecting and examining all the **figures** related to the situation, such as how much, how many, comparisons of prices, averages, frequency and other numerical data.

A basic three-step process to help you be effective in your communication of an issue is:

1. **Get clear** of the situation—find out what happened.

2. **Get the facts**—know all the specifics regarding what happened.

3. **Get specific** in your communication—about the issue.

Many years ago I took my car to my regular auto-mechanic for engine repairs. He quoted the repair at $600. I thought this estimate was pretty high for the type of repair needed, but at that particular moment I had no evidence to back my notion up. So I asked my auto-mechanic about the details of the repair work, including the exact nature and procedure of the repair, which parts are to be replaced, brand name of the replacement parts and warranty conditions. Upon getting this information I told my mechanic that I would think about whether to make the repair. I walked down the street, called two other auto-repair shops in the immediate area, provided all of the specifications my regular mechanic just told me and asked for quotes on the repair. One shop quoted $450, and the other around $500, for the exact same repair!

Now I had specific information to back up my initial notion. Since I liked my regular mechanic, I decided to give him a chance at keeping my business. I went back to the shop and told him about the other two quotes. He was skeptical initially and questioned me about the brand of the parts, as well as the warranty conditions. Since I had done my homework by *getting clear* of the situation and *getting all the facts* straight, I *got specific* in my communication and told him that specifications of the quotes were exactly the same, with price the only difference. Finally, with this *evidence* on my side, I asked him, "So, if you're going to charge me $600 for this repair job, just exactly what am I paying for with that extra money?" He lowered his price to $420.*

In many situations, if you can use "I" language, backed by specific evidence, you put yourself in a fairly good position to work on an issue with another person. However, there will be times when the person you're dealing with is unreasonable, unfair or just downright rude, and no amount of "I" language or evidence will work. In these situations, you should consider setting a consequence.

Such price-comparisons for major services or purchases, naturally, put the consumer in a position of advantage to get the best deal, which is why some businesses refuse to quote prices over the phone. When you are physically in their store and under sales pressure, there is a greater possibility that you will go ahead and make the purchase, even if you're paying a higher price.

How to set consequence

Consequence is what you are willing to do given the situation.

A *good* consequence is one that is significant enough to make the other person think twice about what she/he is doing.

Good communication of a consequence is to offer the other person a *choice*. The four magic words are:

"It's up to you. . . ."

"It's up to you. If you (take course of action A), then (this is my consequence), and if you (take course of action B), then (that is my consequence). You decide."

Many years ago I had an encounter with a rude landlady, who refused to fix broken plumbing in my apartment. At first I tried to *reason* with her by using "I" language ("I would appreciate it if you could take care of this. . ."), backed by evidence of how the plumbing was failing. In spite of my reasonable request, the landlady refused to provide the repair. I decided to set a consequence. "Look, you can do whatever you want to do. Let me tell you what I'm going to do. I'm going to wait until the end of the week for the plumbing to be fixed. If it's not fixed by Saturday, I'm going to call my own plumber; I'm going to have him or her make the repairs, and I'm going to charge his bill against next month's rent. Now you can do whatever you want. THIS is what I'M going to do."

The landlady fixed the plumbing the following day, and since then I haven't had another problem with her.*

Once again, the key to stating a consequence is to give the other person a *choice*, as opposed to saying, "do this or else. . ." which comes across as a threat. When you offer the other person a choice, you are allowing him or her to

---

What would have happened if the landlady continued to refuse the repair? I would have gone ahead and followed up on my stated consequence. One of the fundamental human rights at the beginning of this book states that "we have the right to get what we pay for." Almost every city in the United States has renter protection laws. As a paying

make up his or her own mind, and thus take *ownership* of the decision. It is very important that your consequence is fair and reasonable, and whatever consequences you set, be sure you can back them up with action, if necessary.

Soft on the Person, Tough on the Issue.

"Softer than the flower, where kindness is concerned; stronger than thunder, where principles are at stake."

—Paramhansa Yogananda

In any communication situation, there are two elements present: the relationship you have with this person, and the issue you are discussing. The effective communicator knows how to *separate* the person from the issue, and be soft on the person and tough on the issue.

"Tough mind. Tender Heart."

—Martin Luther King, Jr.

How to be soft on the person

You can be soft on the person by communicating in any of the following ways. These methods can be especially effective if you communicate them before you bring up an issue:

Saying something to affirm the person (mention these only if you believe them to be true):

customer, I had every right to insist on working plumbing in my apartment. What if she insisted on me paying the full rent after I subtracted the repair cost? I would have given her the choice of either dropping her demand or facing me in small claims court, where I would have easily won the case.

25

> "You're a very smart kid. . ."

> "You obviously are very good at this. . ."

Saying something to validate his/her feelings:

> "I know you're not happy about this. . ."

> "I know you're angry with me. . ."

Saying something to affirm your relationship with this person:

> "You are my friend, and as your friend I want to be honest. . ."

> "We've been working together for over a year now. . ."

Speaking toward common goals (find something, *anything,* that both you and the other person can agree on):

> "I know we don't like each other, and I know that we both want to resolve this issue so we can get on with our lives. . ."

> "I'm tired of this, aren't you? Let's get this over with. . ."

How to be tough on the issue

Being tough on the issue simply involves using facts and evidence as discussed earlier in this chapter and, if necessary, back it up with strong (but fair and reasonable) consequence. Once again, evidence, to the extent that they are solid and verifiable, will ground you and keep you strong in your communication. Consequence gives you the leverage (power) to have the other person consider your position and request seriously.

In the first chapter, we talked about how "you" language, when used with directives and universals, is an ineffective way of communicating. There are some exceptions to this, where different types of "you" language can be used to be either soft on the person, or tough on the issue. Let's look at these exceptions now.

Using "you" language to be soft on the person

"You" language plus positive feedback is good for complements:

> "You did a good job on this project!"

> "You are a wonderful cook!"

> "You sing beautifully!"

> "You're really improving!"

Using "you" language in the form of a question to get (or help) the other person come to terms with his or her behavior

In these instances, you are using *behavior and result-focused questioning* to put the other person in a situation where he or she has to come to terms with you (or himself) about his behavior. Behavior and result-focused questioning:

1. Names the observed undesirable behavior, and

2. Confronts the behavior head-on with by using "you" language in the form of a question. Because you are asking a direct question, the likely response of the other person is to address *your* question, instead of continuing a negative behavior. For example:

> "Why are you talking to me like this? Is this the type of behavior I should expect from you?"

> "Are you finished? Because if you're going to keep this up, I'm out of here!"

> "Is this the way you always treat women on a first date? Let me know now!"

27

(Yes, "always" is a universal. In this case, you're using the word deliberately to give the other person a chance to counter with exceptions, and thus refute his or her own undesirable behavior.)

"Are you brave enough to let your guard down with people close to you?"

Behavior and result-focused questioning frequently surprises the other person with how direct and forceful they are, and in their surprise they are much more likely to give pause and re-consider their behavior.

In situations where you ask a question and receive "the run around," repeat the question, followed by "yes or no?" In situations where you get an answer in the negative, now you know better the true nature of the person you're dealing with. This would be a good time to administer a consequence, such as finding a better caliber of people with which to interact.

Using "you" language to interrupt a show of disregard

When someone shows disregard for your concern about an issue, or when someone is acting in a way that is simply unacceptable to you, using "you" language plus *indisputable fact* can be an effective way of disrupting that person's attitude or behavior, and have him or her begin to pay greater attention to the matter. For example:

"You lied to me! You told me that you were going to show up at one o'clock, and you didn't until three!"

"You didn't make the deposit as you said you would!"

"You are being really rude!"

"You just yelled at a kid!"

"You just hit my car!"

Be very careful using "you" language in this way, as it could backfire and intensify a situation. Use this type of "you" language only as an interruption to "shake" a person out of his/ her disregard for your issue, and back it up with indisputable evidence. In addition, communicating in this way in a public situation, where everyone can clearly see and agree with what you're pointing out, can be effective as well. I once saw a receptionist who, in an office full of people, told an obnoxious client, "You're being very rude! Touch me inappropriately again and you'll never become a father!" The client was stunned, apologized and left embarrassed.

Once again, avoid using this type of "you" language excessively, and when you see the other person's negative pattern interrupted, go back to using "I" language and other effective communication skills.

Listen and Validate Feelings

To validate feelings is to recognize the emotions of a person, and to acknowledge that these feelings are really happening to that person. We can validate feelings even if we don't agree with the person or understand the basis for his or her feelings.

Examples of validating feelings:

"I can understand that you feel. . ."

"If I were in your situation, I probably would feel this way too."

"I know you're really upset about this. . ."

"That's terrible! Let's see what we can do. . ."

"I'm sorry to see you so unhappy about this. . ."
(in this example, you're not apologizing. You're
simply saying that you're sorry to see the other
person unhappy).

Caution: Avoid saying, "I know how you feel." This can come across as presumptuous. If the person you're dealing with is showing a clear, specific emotion, name it ("I know you're angry with me. . ."). If the emotion is harder to pinpoint, validate it in more general terms ("I know you're not feeling good about what's happening. . .").

People who work in customer service often say that, when facing a customer with a complaint, to the extent that the customer service representative is willing to listen and say something validating, about half the time the customer will simply walk away without seeking further action. And in cases when the customer doesn't walk away, he is more likely to calm down and discuss the complaint reasonably.

Remember, whenever you encounter a person with negative emotions directed towards you, you have two things with which to deal—this person's negative emotions, and the issue. *Validating feelings can disarm many negative emotions, so that you can focus on the issue.*

CHAPTER THREE

Power Assertion Skills:
The Art of Handling Difficult People

Caution

1. physical safety
   leave the scene & get help.

2. be careful intercultural

3. different skills for different situations

4. practice to build confidence

   Situational power
   1. permanent job military spouse parents/family
   2. temporary.
      Behind aggression / fear
   1. grief, pain
   2. insecurity
   3. vulnerability
   grounded
   1. control
   2. deep breath
   3. soft on person
   4. facts
   5. focus values
   6. human rights
   7. follow up consequences
   8. humor / sarcasm

Definition and Cautions

In this chapter we will identify the mental, emotional, physical and verbal skills that you can use to handle difficult and aggressive people. Appropriately used, these skills can help you deal with difficult or even hostile situations such as intimidation, disrespect, date rape, sexual harassment, sales pressure or physical, emotional or mental abuse.

Please keep the following cautions in mind as you learn power assertion skills:

1. In any hostile situation, your first priority is always to take care of and protect yourself physically, emotionally and mentally. If you do not think you can handle the situation, leave and get help. Choosing NOT to deal with a conflict head-on is one method of conflict resolution. Do NOT use the following communication skills if you don't think you can protect yourself.

2. The following skills are culture-specific to the United States and Canada. They may or may not apply to cultures outside North America.

3. In this section you will find many, many different ways of dealing with very aggressive people. Some of these methods will be more appropriate for some situations than others (dealing with a mugger, obviously, involves a different set of skills than dealing with your insensitive in-law). Depending on your situation and your particular need, pick and use these skills as you see fit.

4. You might find some of these methods a little intimidating to use at first. Confidence comes with practice. Try these skills first in situations where you feel safe, such as with a friend who's obnoxious towards you. As you feel more comfortable with the skills, try them with family members or co-workers. Eventually, you'll build your confidence up so that you will be able to use these skills to protect yourself in very hostile situations.

Let us begin to look now at how to deal with difficult and aggressive people. The first three ideas have to do with mental discipline and self control. The fourth idea involves using words, tone of voice, and body language in hostile situations. The fifth idea involves using humor and sarcasm in certain situations. Many of the ideas in this chapter come from martial arts principles and police training tactics. By developing self-discipline and self-control on the inside, you can better deal with chaos and uncertainty on the outside.

Pick Your Battles

The first thing to consider when you're dealing with a difficult or an aggressive person is to decide if you want to deal with the problem. The principle here is to *pick your battles*, as not all difficult or aggressive people are worth fighting against. Specifically, there are two circumstances under which you might decide not to deal with a situation.

The first circumstance is where someone has temporary, situational power over you. *Situational power* occurs when someone can have power over you in a very limited setting. Usually, as soon as you walk away, this person's power over you is gone. An example would be a rude waiter at a restaurant. If you decide to get a different waiter, or leave the restaurant, this person will no longer have power over you.

Another situation where you might want to think twice about whether you want to deal with a difficult person is when, by temporarily putting up with the aggression, you get something out of it. An example of this would be working a job you hate for six more months, knowing that after six months you will have enough money saved up to go back to school and not work for awhile. Or you might decide to put up with your annoying financial advisor, for although you dislike her, she's really good at finding good investment opportunities for you. So it's worth it to put up with her for a couple of times a year.

In each of the above examples, you're the only one who can decide if the aggressive person or situation is worth fighting about. My suggestion is to think twice, and fight the battles that are truly worth fighting for.

Assuming that you have given the matter some thought, and you decide not to put up with a difficult or an aggressive person, let us discuss now the mental, emotional, physical and verbal tools necessary to help you best handle the situation.

Staying Cool—
The True Nature Behind
Difficult and
Aggressive Behavior

When dealing with a very difficult or aggressive person, remember that even if you are confrontational on the outside, stay cool on the inside.

When we see a person being difficult or acting aggressively, we often recognize external characteristics such as anger, excessive need for control and power, arrogance, manipulation and defensiveness. On the outside, these expressions might seem intimidating and suppressing, as they are meant to be. But when we look deeper into the true nature of such behaviors, we will find that underneath the intimidating and difficult exterior, and behind all the hostile energy, is a set of much more vulnerable emotions.

- Behind excessive, compulsive or pathological anger, we often find a person whose inner life has sadness, pain or grief.

- Behind excessive and overbearing manifestations of control, manipulation, power and arrogance, we commonly find a person who on the inside feels fearful, insecure or inadequate.

35

• Behind excessive defensiveness, we commonly find an inner vulnerability.

Most people who are chronically difficult and/or aggressive do so because they have one or more of these vulnerable "core" emotions on the inside. The core emotions usually have something to do with certain negative experiences from the past. To the extent that a person is unable to face up and deal with his negative experiences, he can sometimes, unconsciously, decide to lash out at others in order to bring a sense of equanimity with his inner fear and pain. By hurting others through aggressive behavior, an aggressive person gets to feel better about him or herself, with the twisted satisfaction that someone else is also suffering. As the old saying goes: "misery loves company." In this twisted way an aggressor's innermost feelings are validated, and he gets to feel better about himself and his own inner suffering.

> *"When you get angry, Hell is born. Anger makes you suffer a lot, and not only do you suffer, but the people you love also suffer at the same time."*
>
> *—Thich Nhat Hanh*

> *"Some people try to be tall by cutting off the heads of others."*
>
> *—Paramhansa Yogananda*

Many excessively difficult and aggressive people are too afraid to be willing to look within and uncover the unpleasant origins of their behavior. It's much easier to hurt others than to examine the true nature of one's own suffering.

Why stay cool in the face of a difficult person? When you lose your cool and get emotional on the inside, you play right into the hands of the aggressor, for you have allowed that person to pull your emotion like a puppet on strings. You give that person the satisfaction of knowing that he or she can

36

have power over you. The aggressor takes delight in seeing you suffer.

When you lose your cool, you become weaker because you are reactive to the aggressor's provocation. You allow your "buttons" to be pushed, and in the process you either sink to the level of the person you're dealing with, or you leave yourself wide open to an aggressor's intimidation, manipulation and exploitation. Stay cool. Don't let others' negative emotions or aggressive behavior get to you.

> *"Use your aggressive feelings boy! Let the hate flow through you. . . . Good! I can feel your anger. . . . Take your weapon, strike me down with all of your hatred, and your journey towards the dark side will be complete!"*
>
> *—The Dark Emperor to Luke Skywalker in "Return of the Jedi"*

How exactly can you stay cool? There are many ways, all of which have to do with keeping yourself grounded.

Keeping Yourself Grounded

Once again, do not let an aggressive person's negative emotions or aggressive behavior get to you. *Focus is the key.* No matter how much the aggressor tries to rattle you, return over and over to focusing on one or more of the following ways of **grounding** yourself. They will keep you cool and composed under pressure:

1. Take deep breaths. Deep breathing calms and grounds.

2. Focus on being soft on the person and tough on the issue.

37

3. Focus on the substance of the issue (facts, figures, hard data).

4. Focus on your principles and values (such as giving and demanding fairness, reasonableness and professionalism).

5. Focus on your fundamental human rights (as listed at the beginning of the book. Insist on being treated with respect, etc.).

6. Offer significant consequence and follow-up if necessary.

7. Use humor and sarcasm (we'll discuss this in detail at the end of this chapter).

Now that we have examined the mental and emotional discipline necessary when confronting an aggressor, lets look at the external communication skills that are important to apply when dealing with aggression.

Powerful Body Language, Words, and Tone of Voice

Direct Eye Contact—in the United States, direct eye contact conveys confidence and strength. Lacking eye contact or frequently looking away are commonly interpreted as a signs of weakness and insecurity. If you are going to confront someone in the U.S., look the person in the eye.

Boundary Gesture—based on how police officers keep suspects from fighting or running away as they make their arrest. The boundary gesture is extending one arm half way out, with the palm of your hand forming a shield tilting slightly downward. This gesture establishes a physical and psychological boundary between you and the other person. This gesture works really well in combination with the words "back off!," both in more soft spoken situations ("could you back off? I need some space.") and in situations, such as date rape, where you want to be very tough and firm ("BACK OFF—NOW!!!").

Power Stance—the power stance simply means that you stand with your feet approximately shoulder width apart as you deal with the aggressor. From many different schools of martial arts, where you are commonly taught how to stand before you learn anything else, we know that standing with your feet shoulder width apart gives you the most physical support and stability. People are literally less able to push you around. And as we feel stronger physically, we also feel stronger and more grounded emotionally and psychologically.

Assertive Commands—these are commands that are intended to stop aggressive behavior. Police officers use many of these commands when apprehending and arresting suspects. You will find almost all of these commands in rape-prevention manuals:

> "NO!"
>
> "STOP!"
>
> "BACK OFF!"
>
> "HOLD IT RIGHT THERE!"
>
> "GO AWAY!"
>
> "DON'T EVEN THINK ABOUT IT!"
>
> ". . . NOW!" (as in "put your hands behind your head NOW!" or "leave NOW!")

In terms of your tone, the best way to say these commands so that the most strength and power come out of your voice is to really emphasize the vowels, and to make them very distinct:

> "nO!"
>
> "stOp!"
>
> "BAAck—OOff!"
>
> "GO—A-wAY!"

Humor and Sarcasm

Humor is a powerful weapon which can:

1. shine light on the truth.

2. show that you are not attached to the situation. Remember, in a conflict situation, the advantage goes to the one who doesn't allow him/herself to be emotionally rattled (or at least doesn't show it). The more you are emotionally caught up in an issue, the more you allow the other person to exploit your attachment to the situation.

Caution:

The following ways of using humor should be used only to *stop* aggression, not to tease people. Those who tease people become aggressors themselves, and will suffer the consequence of all aggressors, namely alienation from people and distance in relationships.

Use humor and sarcasm only if you feel confident and are able to protect yourself in a situation. If you don't feel safe using humor in a situation, do something else. Always take care of and protect yourself as your first priority.

Three ways to use humor and sarcasm

1. **Imitate the aggression.** Literally "act out" his behavior and show the aggressor his own obnoxiousness. When you do this, exaggerate your acting. Be funny and dramatic. Smile and wink as you act out his behavior. When you do this, you are being a mirror which shines on his actions, so that he can see what he is doing.

2. **Exaggerate.** There are two ways to exaggerate:
   1) Exaggerate what he is saying by taking what he says and making it completely ridiculous; and2) Exaggerate yourself as a victim of his aggression. Once again, by exaggerating

the aggressive behavior, you are shining light on the truth, so that he can see what he is doing.

> "You're right, George. These foreigners
> *are* talking about you—*every single one
> of them!*"

> —*The author to his traveling
> companion in China*

3. **Opposite.** Here you take the aggressive or a negative behavior and compliment the opposite. For example, you can tell a foul-mouthed teenager what a well-mannered and polite person she is, or someone who's extremely impatient that you really like her because of her patience, or call a man who's a pain "Mr. Wonderful."

These ideas are what I call "in your face" communication. They are direct, and yet they make a point without you getting too serious or worked up about the issue.

Possible reactions from difficult or aggressive people when you use humor and sarcasm

They are temporarily shocked, surprised, thrown off balance, or don't know what to do.

Your response: You have succeeded in interrupting their aggression. Focus on the issue immediately, and be soft on the person as you validate their feelings. ("I know it's not easy. . . ," "I know you're upset, and I might be too if I were in your situation. . . .")

They become angrier and more controlling, intimidating or demanding.

Sometimes, when those who rely on anger/intimidation/ abuse of power to get what they want or feel their aggression challenged, their response is to intensify their efforts in order to maintain control over you and the situation.

Your response: You have succeeded in pushing their buttons. Keep using humor appropriately and keep offering them an option (a face-saving back door for them) by telling them you are ready to talk about the issue whenever they are. Most people will calm down and start to become more cooperative after sensing their little tirade is not going to work. If they don't stop the aggression, tell them that you refuse to deal with them until they can calm down and communicate to you in a reasonable manner, then leave.

They start laughing *with* you.

Your response: This is the best response you can hope for. People who can laugh together can work together. Go immediately to working on the issue and be soft on the person.

They walk away, bolt out the door.

You have succeeded in interrupting their aggression so well that they can't handle you anymore.

Your response: Decide under the circumstances if it's best to go after them or talk to them after they have calmed down. In either case, be soft on the person the next time you see them, then focus on the issue.

CHAPTER FOUR

Conflict Resolution:
A Step-by-Step Guide

.

Problem Statement

Think about a situation in your life where you are experiencing conflict, aggression, unfair treatment, hostility or disrespect. Describe this situation in detail. If you can't think of such a situation in your life right now, recall a situation from the past that you would like to examine:

_____

_____

_____

_____

_____

_____

_____

_____

_____

_____

_____

_____

_____

_____

_____

_____

_____

_____

(continue next page if necessary)

FINAL

Understanding the Nature of Power

Two major categories of power

Tangible power—when someone can administer a physical, informational, financial and/or material consequence on you.

This power is *tangibly real,* as people with this power in your life can influence the quality of your life.

Emotional power—when you regard a person with strong emotional feelings (positive or negative), you allow this person to have power over you.

This power is *perceived* (created by you, not the other party). Your *attitude* or your way of thinking and feeling towards this person determines whether this person has any power over you. *A change in your attitude can neutralize and/or negate this power.*

Seven specific types of power under the two categories

French and Raven, in their work. *The Basics of Social Power,*[1] identified the following five types of power.

1. **Legitimate Power**—power that comes with title or position.

2. **Reward Power**—When you think that someone can reward you tangibly and/or emotionally, this person has power over you. *We grant them the power.*

3. **Punishment Power**—When you think someone can punish you tangibly and/or emotionally, this person has power over you. *police*

4. **Referent Power**—When you look up to, admire, like or love a person because of what you see in this person, this person has referent power over you. *Man of the cloth, movie star — famous people.*

similar in relationship

47

5. **Expert Power**—People who have (or profess to have)
   knowledge or expertise that you don't, can have expert
   power over you. *Doctors lawyers, scientists etc.*

In addition, there are these two types of power:

6. **Loathsome Power**—When you have anger, hate or fear
   toward a person, you are vulnerable to this person pushing
   your "hot buttons." This can cause you to be reactive and
   lose your cool. This person has power over you because you
   let him/her effect you in a negative way. Your negative
   emotions, although perhaps justifiable, nevertheless, leave
   you emotionally vulnerable. *Your hate of someone consumes you.*

7. **Situational Power**—People who can give you a hard
   time in a very specific situation can have situational
   power over you. An example would be a rude waiter at a
   restaurant. If you decide to get a different waiter or leave the
   restaurant, this person will no longer have power over you.
   Temporary – permanent

Absolute power over me in this country

1. 1. J. R. P. French and B. H. Raven, "The Basis of Social Power," in D.
   Cartwright and A. Zander (eds.), *Group Dynamics* (Evanston, Illinois:
   Row, Peterson, 1962), pp. 607-623.

Power Dynamic Analysis

Let's examine the situation you have written and determine its power dynamics (significant power = enough power to influence/change another person's action/behavior).
Check all that apply:

Type of Power	Others have significant emotional power over you in this area	You have significant emotional power over others in this area	Others have significant tangible power over you in this area	You have significant tangible power over others in this area
1. Legitimate	N/A	N/A		
2. Reward				
3. Punishment				
4. Referent			N/A	N/A
5. Expert				
6. Loathsome			N/A	N/A
7. Situational				

Exercise continued on the next page ☞

Based on your checklist, answer the following questions:

1. Who has more overall emotional power in this situation? (circle)

   You   Other(s)   Both   Not Applicable

2. Who has more overall tangible power in this situation? (circle)

   You   Other(s)   Both   Not Applicable

3. Is the power in this situation predominately emotional or tangible? (circle)

   Predominately   Predominately   Both Equally
   Emotional   Tangible   Predominate

- If predominately emotional, go to page 51.
- If predominately tangible, go to page 52.
- If both equally predominant, read page 51 first, then go to page 52 and complete your analysis.

Dealing With Predominately Emotional Situations

If you have more emotional power:

Use **Effective Communication Skills** to communicate to this person and deal with the situation. In the great majority of cases, Effective Communication Skills will help you get your point across and be understood. Since you have more emotional power in this situation, there is no need to "overkill" by using Power Assertion Skills, which are more confrontational and "get in their face." *Remember, be soft on the person, tough on the issue.* Set a tangible/emotional consequence only if absolutely necessary. If you do so, be sure that you are reasonable, fair and clear in your communication of your intentions and your reasons for doing so.

Your **leverage** (what gives you power in this situation): State emotional/tangible consequence (only if necessary).

If you both have significant emotional power over each other:

Use **Effective Communication Skills,** plus **Power Assertion Skills** as needed and appropriate. The latter should be used only if the other person is being aggressive, unreasonable or disrespectful towards you. If the other person is sincerely trying to come to an understanding or a resolution with you, then Effective Communication Skills alone should be adequate.

Your **leverage** (what gives you power in this situation): Staying cool, emotional detachment, state emotional/tangible consequence and be willing to follow through, if necessary.

If the other person has more emotional power:

First of all, remember that emotional power is a matter of perception. This person has no power over you except for what you give him/her emotionally due to your perception of this person. When you stop giving emotional power (positive or negative) to this person, this person will no longer have emotional power over you.

Use both **Effective Communication Skills** and **Power Assertion Skills** in this situation. The latter should be used only if the other person is being aggressive or disrespectful towards you. When he/she becomes more reasonable, then use only **Assertive Communication Skills.** If all else fails, agree that you disagree and follow up on your stated consequence.

Your **leverage** (what gives you power in this situation): Staying cool, emotional detachment, state emotional/tangible consequence and be willing to follow through if necessary.

Dealing With Predominately Tangible Situations

If you have more tangible power:

Use **Effective Communication Skills** to communicate to this person and deal with the situation. In the great majority of cases, Effective Communication Skills will help you get your point across and be understood. Since you have more tangible power in this situation, there is no need to "overkill" by using Power Assertion Skills, which are more confrontational and "get in their face." *Remember, be soft on the person, tough on the issue.* Set a tangible/emotional consequence only if absolutely necessary. If you do so, be sure that you are reasonable, fair and clear in your communication of your intentions and your reasons for doing so.

Your **leverage** (what gives you power in this situation): State emotional/tangible consequence (only if necessary).

If you both have significant tangible power over each other:

Use **Effective Communication Skills,** plus **Power Assertion Skills** as needed and appropriate. The latter should be used only if the other person is being aggressive, unreasonable or disrespectful towards you. If the other person is sincerely trying to come to an understanding or a resolution with you, then Effective Communication Skills alone should be adequate.

Your **leverage** (what gives you power in this situation): Staying cool, emotional detachment, state tangible consequence and be willing to follow through, if necessary.

If the other person has more tangible power:

First, try communicating to this person using **Effective Communication Skills.** Remember to use "I" language backed by specific facts and evidence. Do not use Power Assertion Skills at this time, except for *staying cool* and *staying grounded.*

If this doesn't work, then withdraw yourself from the situation temporarily, and ask yourself the following the questions:

1. Do I get something out of putting up with this situation that benefits me?

2. Is it worth it for me to put up with this situation?

Sometimes, we put up with people's aggressiveness or unreasonableness because we know we are getting something out of the situation. (For example, temporarily staying in your unpleasant old job until you get a new job, or putting up with a rude administrative clerk because you just want to get what you want and then get out of there.) If this is the case, especially if the aggressiveness or unreasonableness is temporary or situational, then you may decide not to make the situation an issue. Remember, in these situations you are neither stuck nor powerless, you are simply making a *choice* in order to get what you want.

Similarly, sometimes it's simply not worth dealing with the aggression or unreasonableness because in the larger picture, it's not worth fighting about. You can use the *percentage rule* to help you decide. For example, if your roommate is great 90% of the time, but a real pain in the neck 10%, you *might* decide to put up with the situation because you like the 90%. In the bigger, total picture, it might not be that bad. The key is to pick your battles, and fight only those battles worth fighting for.

With this in mind, answer these two questions:

1. Do I get something out of putting up with this situation that benefits me?   Yes   No

2. Is it worth it for me to put up with this situation?
                            Yes   No

If you answered **yes** to *one or both* questions, then you know that you are putting up with the situation for a reason. Keep your sight on your goal (what you get out of the situation) and let things be. If the situation becomes unbearable, then go back to the two questions again and re-evaluate.

Your **leverage** (what gives you power in this situation):
Focus on obtainment of your worthwhile goal.

If you answered *no* to **both** questions, then this situation really doesn't have any tangible power over you because your answers are stating that *you gain nothing important* by staying in this situation. You have nothing to lose by dealing with the situation directly and assertively. Use **Effective Communication Skills,** plus **Power Assertion Skills** as needed and appropriate. The latter should be used only if the other person is being aggressive, unreasonable or disrespectful towards you. If the other person is sincerely trying to come to an understanding or a resolution with you, then Effective Communication Skills alone should be adequate.

Your **leverage** (what gives you power in this situation):
Staying cool, emotional detachment, state tangible consequence, and be willing to follow through, if necessary.

54

Brainstorm Solutions

What thoughts, feelings and insights occurred to you as you went through the preceding pages? What have you learned about your stated situation so far?

Write down some possible ways of dealing with your stated situation. This is a brainstorming session. Write down all the different possibilities you can think of to handle your situation, even if they contradict each other.

_____

_____

_____

_____

_____

_____

_____

_____

_____

_____

_____

_____

_____

_____

_____

_____

_____

(continue next page if necessary)

_____

_____

_____

_____

_____

_____

_____

_____

_____

_____

_____

_____

_____

_____

_____

_____

_____

_____

_____

_____

_____

_____

_____

_____

_____

(continue next page if necessary)

Identity Solution

Now that you have a list of possible solutions from the brainstorm, write down what you think is the best way to deal with your stated situation. Be specific. State the attitude, communication, consequence and action steps necessary to accomplish your goal.

_____

_____

_____

_____

_____

_____

_____

_____

_____

_____

_____

_____

_____

_____

_____

_____

_____

_____

(continue next page if necessary)

Bits and Pieces

*People. People important to you, people
unimportant to you cross your life, touch it
with love and carelessness and move on.
There are people who leave you and you
breathe a sigh of relief and wonder why you
ever came into contact with them. There are
people who leave you and you breath a sign
of remorse and wonder why they had to go
away and leave such a gaping hole. Children
leave parents, friends leave friends.
Acquaintances move on. People change
homes. People grow apart. Enemies hate and
move on. Friends love and move on. You
think of the many who have moved into your
hazy memory. You look on those present
and wonder.*

*I believe in God's master plan in lives. . . . He
moves people in and out of each other's lives,
and each leaves his mark on the other. You
find you are made up of bits and pieces of all
who ever touched your life, and you are more
because of it, and you would be less if they
had not touched you.*

*Pray God that you accept the bits and pieces
in humility and wonder, and never question
and never forget.*

—Anonymous

A Note of Appreciation

My sincere thanks to José Yulo for the introduction; Karen Rosen for content editing; Shelley Schreiber for content layout and design; Ronnie Griese for production editing and proofreading; and the students at Foothill College for their invaluable input and support.

Notes

Notes

Notes